Intimate Conversations
With God

Early Prayers of a New Christian

Intimate Conversations With God

Early Prayers of a New Christian

Latrea Wyche

Copyright

Copyright © 2017 by Latrea Wyche. All rights reserved. This book or any portion thereof may not be reproduced or used in any manner whatsoever without the express written permission of The Butterfly Typeface Publishing House Co. except for the use of brief quotations in a book review.

Scripture quotations taken from the 21st Century King James Version @, copyright 1994. (KJ21) Used by permission of Deuel Enterprises, Inc., Gary, SD 57237. All rights reserved.

Printed in the United States of America

First Printing, 2017

ISBN-13: 978-1-942022-83-1

ISBN10: 1942022832

The Butterfly Typeface Publishing
PO BOX 56193
Little Rock, Arkansas 72215

This book is dedicated to anyone who has been on a quest to find a deeper, more meaningful and fulfilling relationship with God, but hasn't known how to accomplish this.

This book is also for anyone who longs to understand prayer and the role it plays in our walk with God.

Table of Contents

Introduction 14
    A Willing Spirit 15
Why We Pray 19
    An Invitation 20
    A Relationship 22
Types of Prayers 25
    Supplication 28
    Petition 29
    Thanksgiving 30
Grace 31
My Prayers 35
    Reflection on purpose 38
Strongholds 39
    Stronghold Prayers 43
    Reflection on Strongholds 46
Consecration 49
More prayers 67
    Reflection on Deliverance 96
Unanswered Prayers 100
    Reflection on Praying 107
Conclusion 108
    Surrender 109
About the Author 111

Foreword

These prayers played an instrumental part to the woman that I am today because they were prayed during a time in my life where I knew something needed to change and I knew God wanted more from me than the road that I was traveling. However, for some reason, I did not know how to tap into it. It was like this wall was up and no matter how hard I tried, I just could not move forward.

It always seemed to me as if everyone else had a deeper connection with God then what I had. I yearned for an intimate relationship with Him as well.

Since then, God has shown me that everyone has their own relationship with Him. No one has the exact same type of relationship.

I liken it to a parent who has more than one child. As those children get older, the parents discover that they have over time, developed a different relationship with each child.

Don't get me wrong, I don't mean that one parent loves one child more than the other(s), what I mean is that the parent tends to communicate or relate to each child differently.

I believe God does the same with us.

-Latrea Wyche

Acknowledgment

I would like to acknowledge and thank everyone who has helped me along this journey.

First and foremost, I would like to thank God for giving me the gift, grace and the knowledge to write such a book which was not very easy at all.

Second I would like to thank my baby cakes, my daughter Olivia; the best thing that has ever happened to me and my biggest cheerleader. Mommy always loves you.

Next I would like to thank Mr. Barry Wyche. I want to thank you for putting up with me when you did not have to. We've been through a lot, and yet you are still here.

And last, but not least, I want to thank *Breath of God* Sunday School Department. This book was birthed from our many conversations about prayer. I love you guys.

Latrea Wyche

Intimate Conversations ...

Introduction

A Willing Spirit

As I was preparing to write this book, it was my assumption that God just wanted me to write a book of my prayers. Then God was like, "How you gonna write about something so important as prayer and not lay a foundation?"

Then I was like, "But God (I don't know about you guys but this is how I talk to God), I don't want *my* book to be like every other prayer book out there."

He replied, "There can be a million prayer books on the shelves, but there is only going to be one written by Latrea Wyche, and that is all that you need to be concerned with. You write the book the way I tell you to write it and let me do the rest."

Well he didn't have to tell me more than once, so here we go.

I often tell my Sunday school students this all the time when I ask them to pray in class, "So many times, we want to make the things of God so complicated. All God requires of us is to come to Him with a willing spirit and a heart of repentance, and let Him do the rest."

So many times, when we pray, we get caught up in if we are doing it *right*; are we using the *right* words, and are we saying the *right* things. I truly believe that when the people of God finally reach the understanding that all prayer really is ... is just an intimate conversation with God. There is no *right* or *wrong* way to pray.

Because God knew us before we were conceived in our mother's womb, that means He knows what we stand in the need of before we even open our mouths. Why do we come to God like He does not know what's going on with us? I mean sometimes we pray like God has no idea who we are and or what we are going through.

For example, if your rent is due the 3rd of every month and God has made a way for you to pay it on time every month, why are you still praying about your rent every month? Like one month He is just going to decide to go on vacation and not make a way for you the way He has been doing all the other months.

The question I often get from my Sunday School children is this, "If God already knows what we need, then why do we pray? Why doesn't He just bless us?" Quiet as it is kept, some adults ponder the same thing.

I was raised believing that prayer was just one of those things you did and no one ever really explained why you should pray. I mean of course we all heard the saying, *Prayer changes things*, and there has never been a more truer statement, but I have always felt there was deeper meaning behind the act of prayer.

After being faced with the question from my Sunday School children, and my own curiosity, I decided to do some research on *why* we should pray.

*Intimate Conversations ...*

Why We Pray

Based on my research the number one reason we pray is to not only invite God into our lives, but to invite Him into our situations as well. God is not a rude God. He will not just barge into a situation. He is going to stand on the side and wait to be invited in, and if we never invite Him in then He will continue to stand on the sideline.

An Invitation

I've been in situations when for whatever reason, it was just not working out in my favor and I could not understand why.

What was I doing wrong?

It felt like no matter what I did, the situation was still not working out in my favor. The key word here is "I". I tried to work it out on my own. I tried to figured it out, and I was not inviting God into the situation.

But sure enough as soon as I went to God about it, not only did I feel a sense of relief, but the situation began to work out the way I needed it to.

The funny thing I learned about God is that He is like a parent with a child. You remember how when you were a child you wanted to do it yourself and your parents would step aside and let you try it yourself knowing in the back of their minds that you will need some help, but they let you try anyway.

God is the same way. He will step back and let us practically make a mess of our situations. Then when we finally decide to come to Him it's like He is saying, "Ok are you ready for my help now?"

One thing we tend to do, even when we give a situation to God, is when we feel like He is not moving fast enough or He is not working it out the way *we* want Him to, we take the situation back.

God being who He is. He will give it right back to us like, "Ok, if you think you are better at this than me, take your best shot." In most cases, we just end up where we started and God is still standing on the sidelines like, "When you are really ready to completely give it to me, I will be here waiting."

A Relationship

Another reason we pray is to build a relationship with God. With any relationship, there must be some communication. It's like a plant, in order for that plant to grow it requires certain things like water and sunlight. That's the same thing with our relationship with God we must communicate with Him on a regular basis in order for our relationship with Him to grow.

This is something that I would often struggle with, being consistent with my prayer life. I would do good for a while. Every morning before I did anything, I would go to my prayer area with my worship music and spend a good 45 minutes to an hour first praising and worshiping God, and then I would go into prayer. I'm telling you when I would get finished it felt like a weight had been lifted off my shoulders and my day would be great. I felt great.

I would be good and on track for about a week, then I would allow one thing to throw me off track and before I know it

I would start to feel different in my spirit. I would not feel bad, but I would not feel God like I did when I was praying like He called me to do.

It took me a minute to make the connection, but soon I realized that the less I pray, the less connected I felt to God. However, the more I prayed the more I could feel Him in my spirit.

The wonderful thing I love about God is even though we may stop listening from time to time, He never stops talking.

*Intimate Conversations ...*

Types of Prayers

The different types of prayers are something else that I have wondered about.

After this book was written, the Lord told me to go back and include this information. I learned about the different types of prayers while writing this book.

Even though I had prayed my whole life, I never knew there were different types of prayers and they were based on your situation.

By being within the body of Christ, I have heard these terms before, but I never really knew what they meant.

Side note: Never be afraid to do your own research. If you hear a word during bible study or during Sunday Service, write it down and go home and research it. God wants us to understand His word. The Bible tells us to "Study to shew thyself approved unto God...". **(2 Timothy 2:15 KJV)**

Based on my research, I found there are three types of prayers: supplication, petition and thanksgiving.

Supplication

One type of prayer is the **Prayer of Supplication.** Again, I have heard this phrase before, but I had no idea what it meant. So, I looked it up.

By definition, supplication is *a humble request for help from someone in authority.*

So, when we make requests on behalf of ourselves to God, that is the prayer of supplication.

"And my God will supply every need of yours according to his riches in glory in Christ Jesus." **(Philippians 4:19 ESV)**

In the above verse, there is a request being made for God to supply all of my needs according to His riches and glory.

Petition

Another type of prayer, the **Prayer of Petition** or intercessory prayer is the action of pleading on someone else's behalf.

When someone says, "I am interceding on behalf of this person," that means they are going to God in prayer on behalf of that person.

"For where two or three are gathered in my name, there am I among them." **(Matthew 18:20 ESV)**

Thanksgiving

The third type of prayer is the **Prayer of Thanksgiving**.

In my opinion, this is the prayer that we tend to pray the least. With this prayer, we are not asking God for anything, we are simply thanking Him.

We thank Him not only for what He has done and continue to do in our lives, but we are also thanking Him for who He is to us and who He is in our lives.

This type of prayer can be as simple as saying, "I thank my God in all my remembrance of you." **(Philippians 1:3 ESV)**

Latrea Wyche

Intimate Conversations ...

Grace

Grace is defined as the undeserved acceptance and love given to us by God.

Often, we hear people pray and they thank God for His grace and mercy, but they may not *really* know what they are thanking God for. My question is, do people *really* know what it means to pray for grace? A lot of times we just say what we hear other believers say and it becomes a catch phrase.

Grace is knowing that God's love has no end and no limit. There is absolutely nothing we can ever conceive of that would make God stop loving us. I don't know about you but that makes me happy today.

Let me be clear before I go any further. There may come a time in your life where God may have to take his hands off you. That does not mean He won't be there to catch you, that just means that you were not listening and repeatedly choosing to live in sin.

So God is like, ok I have warned you of what would happen if you continued to live the way you choose, I guess I just I have to show and he will take is hands off of you but like most parents He will always love you.

On these next few pages, I will share with you some of my prayers (intimate conversations) that I've had with God.

As the subtitle suggests, these are the prayers of a *new* Christian. I'd like to think I've grown since then.

It was important for me to share my early thoughts as a 'new Christian' because I realize that some of you may have had the same thoughts or been in similar situations.

I want you to know that every day is a new day and a new opportunity to try it again.

Latrea Wyche

Intimate Conversations ...

My Prayers

Dear God,

I come to you with repentance in my heart. For I have been very selfish this weekend. I attended a *Women In Leadership* retreat and when I first decided to go, I thought it would be a great idea to do something that would get me closer to God. However, when I got there I started feeling bad because I after only the first night, I convinced myself that I wasn't going to get anything from this retreat.

So most of the weekend, I moped around like a spoiled child thinking, "What am I going to get out of this?"

After praying the whole weekend for direction and understanding in this situation, it was not until the last day of the retreat that you spoke to me.

This is what you told me:

"This retreat was not about *you* getting anything from it. You were sent to support your first Lady and be *her* blessing."

After hearing that, I felt like my eyes were open. So I ask you right now in your holy name for your forgiveness for my selfishness.

Amen.

Reflection on purpose

As I look back on the previous prayer, I realize this was about me trying to find my purpose within God. It was like I was turning over every leaf looking for some type of sign that I was in the right place, that I was where God wanted me to be and that I was not a waste.

This situation taught me that it not always about me. Sometimes, God will put us in places to be used and we don't even know that we are being used.

I think so many times we think to be *used* by God means we have to hold some big office or be on some board. However, He could use you just as a ladder holder, for someone else to get their blessing.

Latrea Wyche

Intimate Conversations ...

Strongholds

Strongholds have been chasing me all my life. It was not until I read Denise Boggs' *Book of Prayers* did I discover what a stronghold was.

Boggs defines a stronghold as a "generational curse created by the devil and passed down from generation to generation to keep families in bondage."

One example of a generational curse or stronghold that I have had to fight with is the spirit of lust. I did not even know that I had this stronghold or where it came from until I got married and I saw these weird tendencies start to show up. I had no idea where they came from, but once I read the Bible and I looked up my family heritage I began to understand.

My birth mother had problems within her marriage and she had two kids by two different men. Her mother also had the same issue. I started to see the pattern and according to the Bible the only cure for strongholds is prayer and fasting.

"For the weapons of our warfare are not of the flesh but have (ESV) divinely powerful for the destruction of fortresses." (AMP) **(2 Corinthians 10:4)**

Strongholds cause the people of God to interpret life based on a false reality and not on the truth found in God's word. For example, you may have grown up in a family that was poor and because everyone in that family before you operated out of lack, you somehow believe that you have to operate out of that same lack.

But you have to learn to use the word of God as your weapon, "You are a lender and not a borrower, you are head and never the tail." **(Deuteronomy 28:12)**

The more you start to speak these things into the atmosphere, the more you will notice that your mindset will change and you will see strongholds start to break off your life.

Latrea Wyche

Intimate Conversations ...

Stronghold Prayers

Dear God,

In the name of Jesus, I hereby bind any and all strongholds that have ever been spoken over my life. I will be everything that you have placed in me to be. I shall walk in the anointing that you placed on my life since my conception. When I become weary, I ask that you send your holy spirt to remind me of your promises. I ask that you cast the lies and word curses that have been spoken over me by myself and others back to the pits of hell in which they come from. In your son's name.

                                                Amen.

Latrea Wyche

Dear God,

I come to you lost and confused about my marriage. I feel like I'm at the end of my rope and I don't know what to do. I love my husband and he means the world to me, but I need intimacy and he does not seem to understand that. So today I ask that you help heal our marriage take me off the chat line because I know that this is not of you or your will for my life. I know that I should only be talking to my husband in a sexual nature, but I feel stuck. There are certain things that I desire and he refuses to give them to me. I am crying out for you to help me and I know you are the only one who can help at this point. In Jesus name, I pray.

Amen.

Reflection on Strongholds

I feel that I have prayed these stronghold prayers time and time again. At first I thought God did not hear me or He was just ignoring me because it seemed that the more I prayed the worst it got. I was like, "What gives God? I know I am not the only one out there that has felt this way."

Have you ever prayed to God for Him to fix or remove something and it seemed the more you prayed the harder that situation got?

It was not I read **(2 Corinthians 12:9 ESV)** did I get clarity. Here Paul is talking to God asking Him to remove the thorn from his flesh and God replies, "My grace is sufficient for you, for my power is made perfect in weakness." Therefore I will boast all the more gladly about my weaknesses, so that Christ's power may rest on me.

From this verse, I have come to understand that there are somethings that God is not going to fix or remove because he wants use to rely on His grace during our moments of weakness.

Latrea Wyche

There can be a million prayer books on the shelves, but there is only going to be one written by Latrea Wyche...

Intimate Conversations ...

Consecration

These next set of prayers are prayers that I prayed during the time of consecration. In some areas, you are going to see where I have added Bible verses because we were told to read a certain book during this time.

I wrote down the verse that stuck out to me and used it during my prayer time. But what was I hoping to gain from this consecration was direction so I always think it's a good idea so set some goals before starting something like this.

What I hope to gain from this experience:

- Wisdom **(Acts 6:10)**
- Understanding **(Jeremiah. 3:15, Luke 2:4)**
- Direction **(Proverbs 3:6)**
- Spiritual Growth

Dear God,

In the precious name of Jesus, I ask that during this quiet time with you that you cleanse my heart, remove anything that is unlike you, and use this time to open my eyes to the things which are seen. Allow me to learn my purpose in you, allow me to find direction and wisdom in your word. I seek after you with my whole heart. I just want my steps to line up with yours. In Jesus name I pray.

Amen.

Dear God,

First and foremost, let me give you all the honor and praise to you and your Holy name. I am on day five of this fast. Physically I feel terrible, but spiritually I feel somethings are being renewed within me. My husband told me I looked weak and needed to eat, but I know that what my flesh is going through means that you are tearing somethings down and getting rid of somethings that are not like you. So I am going to stick with it until the end. I know you have great things in store for me and my family. I can feel it. I just have to continue to be faithful to your word.

Amen.

Latrea Wyche

Dear God,

The day is done and I want to say thank you for allowing me to see another day in your glorious name. I thank you for all your wonderful blessings even the ones I can't see for I know they will all work out for the good of your name, I pray.

Amen.

Dear God,

I come to you, first thanking you for all the many blessing you have bestowed upon me and my family. You are a God that see and knows all todays. I come in prayer not for myself, but for my mother. Lord, I ask that you become the angel on her shoulder and the voice of reason that guides her in the darkness. When she feels like she can't carry the weight of this world, I ask that you will be her calm in the storm. I also send up a prayer of protection for my family. Keep your hedge of protection over them as they navigate through life.

Amen.

Latrea Wyche

"Have mercy on me,
O God according to your steadfast love;
according to your abundant mercy,
bot out my transgressions.
Wash me thoroughly from my iniquity,
and cleanse me for my sins!"
Psalms 51:1-2 (ESV)

Dear God,

I come to you with a spirit of repentance. I have not been as committed as I should have been during this fast. The first week I must say I thought I was going to die of hunger, but that was okay because I was in my Word and saying my prayers every morning. I mean, I was really impressed with how well I was doing.

But along the way something happened and I started to fall off it like I was losing my faith in all that you have revealed to me. I could not understand why this was happening, I mean everything was crystal clear to me at one point ... then I discovered the root cause; the less I prayed and read my word the less I will feel connected to you.

So, I come to you asking for forgiveness in not giving you the time that you deserve, in Jesus name.

Amen.

Latrea Wyche

Dear God,

As I ride to Bible study, I am in a state of confusion not really knowing who and where I fit in your kingdom. I am trying hard to find my place. I know you have a place created specifically for me, but I just don't know how to tap into it. It is my prayer that you make me the strong woman of God that you would have to me to be. Oh Lord, I cry out to you. I feel so lost and confused.

Amen.

Dear God,

I know it's been a while since you have heard from me. I really don't have an excuse as to why but I do know this:

There is a lot about life that at age thirty-two I don't understand, but with you and your guidance, all things will be revealed to me on your time not mine.

I have to trust you and your word. You have never left my side even when I did not deserve your grace, you still blessed me.

I come to you tonight as humble as I know how. There are no words that could express how much I love and want to be close to you.

Latrea Wyche

That is my prayer tonight - a closer walk with you. I want to be all that you want me to be.

I want your will to be done. My will may not be the same as your will for me, but I know your will is to take my life and shape it into what you want it to be.

Amen.

Latrea Wyche

Dear God,

I thank you Lord, for allowing me to see a new day, to breathe your wonderful air. I ask that today be the day you order my steps, let my words be your words and let your thoughts be my thoughts. This is my prayer for this day.

Amen.

Latrea Wyche

Dear God,

It's me again, sometimes I feel like I am bothering you, especially when I am praying for the same thing all the time. For me the strange thing is I know you can release me from the things that are not of you, but for some reason you won't and I don't understand why. I know that you are an all-powerful God and you do what you want when you want to, but this spirit that I have is not of you. It has caused me to lie, be selfish, sin against you and your name sake. You have been too good to me. In Jesus name I pray.

Amen.

Dear God,

It is my desire to follow you with all of my heart, soul, mind and strength. Please help me see any area in my life in which I have intentionally or unintentionally allowed compromise to creep in. Today I recommit my life completely to you.

Awaken my soul and fill me with your presence.

Lord, there is a situation that I have been dealing with for a while. I have asked you to release me from it time and time again and I don't understand why I can't shake this thing.

Am I not praying enough?

Am I not praying the right prayers?

Please God, I need some type of sign. I know that this behavior in not of you, but then why won't you release me from it?

I know you can; it's never been a question of if, but will you?

Amen.

Latrea Wyche

Dear God,

I pray that today I would have the kind of resolve to lay my burdens at your feet.

I am faced with so much and I know that you care about every last detail of my life.

Create a testimony though my experiences that will reach others in some way, shape or form while bringing you the glory that you deserve.

Amen.

Latrea Wyche

Dear God,

I thank you for the Holy Spirit that guides and prompts me in your ways. Thank you that you have never left me or forsaken me. Help me to always choose your ways over mine, for your ways are higher than mine.

Amen.

Latrea Wyche

Intimate Conversations ...

More prayers

So many times we become so wrapped up in what we want and the things that we are only permitted to see with our corneal eyes that we forget who is really in control.

Even though we may not be able to see it in the midst of the situation, God's way is always going to be better than our ways. No matter what the situation is that we may come against.

A lot of times we may not understand God's plan or His direction. To be honest I don't really think God cares whether we understand it or not. I don't even think he care if we like it.

All God is really concerned with is do we have enough faith in who he is to be obedient even when we don't know the plan?

Can we still follow Him when there is no light?

That is a question you really need to ask yourself can you still follow God when you have no idea what is going on or what He is trying to do.

Latrea Wyche

Dear God,

I thank you for the Holy Spirit that guides me and prompts me in all of your ways. Thank you that you never left me nor forsake me. Help me to always choose your ways above my own ways, for your ways will always be better than mine.

Amen.

Latrea Wyche

Dear God,

On this day Lord I want to say thank you for allowing me to see yet another year. You did not have to do it and I just want to say thank you.

I have had so much negativity spoken into my life on how I was not expected to make it or I was not going to be anything. According to You and your word no weapon formed against me shall prosper and that is the word that I stand on today.

Today was my 33rd birthday and at this stage of my life, I am so confused. I knew that I wanted more of God, but I did not know how to tap into His presence the way I needed to. Plus I was still doing some things that I knew that I should not have been doing.

Latrea Wyche

I felt trapped because it's was like I was doing these things because I felt like it was what I needed to do at the time even though they were wrong.

I still felt like there was this wall up that I just could not tap through no matter how hard I tried.

Amen.

Latrea Wyche

Dear God,

Open my eyes to see that your ways lead only to life. I will trust you with all of my heart. Thank you that you Grace empowers me to walk in your ways. Thank you that I have not been left to my own ability, but empowered to live in a way I could never live on my own.

Amen.

Dear God,

I pray that today you use me to speak encouragement to others and work to uplift them in their time of need. Strengthen me with the boldness to pray with people in need.

It is my prayer Lord that you continue to allow me to operate in the boldness of your word. I am reminded that our weapons of the flesh are carnal, they are not of the spirit.

As I typed this prayer, tears began to roll down my eyes because the one thing that I have always wanted to do - the one thing that I would always ask God to allow me to do - I am finally doing.

When you pray for something you have to trust that if it's within the will of God it shall come to pass.

"For the vision is yet for an appointed time, but at the end it shall speak, and not lie: though it tarry, wait for it; because it will surely come, it will not tarry." **(Habakkuk 2:3 KJV)**

What I was asking God for was for an appointed time, and even though I thought I was ready when I was asking for the blessing God felt otherwise.

Amen.

Latrea Wyche

"The fear of a man brings a snare"

Proverbs 29:25 (AMP)

Latrea Wyche

Dear God,

I pray when I am afraid of others and of their opinions of me, I choose to trust in you. I honor you above any other. Thank you for peace and freedom from the fear of man and his opinion.

Amen.

Latrea Wyche

Dear God,

Putting my name on your plan is like Saul putting his armor on David. Please don't ever let me try to cover what you are doing. Let me be transparent so that you will always get the glory.

Amen.

Latrea Wyche

Dear God,

I come to you in prayer first to just say thank you for your very presence in my life. You have always been my rock even when I did not know that you were there, you were there. For that I thank you, Lord. I yearn to be in your grace. I yearn to follow your word.

Throughout this fast I was determined I was going to do what I needed to do to seek your face unlike ever before and even though I am only midway through it, I feel so much closer to you.

Yokes are being broken. I am now ready as I am armed with the boldness of your word. I am ready to take my rightful place in your army as one of your footmen.

Amen.

Latrea Wryche

Dear God,

I thank you for all that you have done for me and are continuing to do in my life. Help me to acknowledge You in all your ways and receive your grace in everything that I do.

Allow my life to bring glory to your name, as you empower me to advance in your kingdom.

Lord as I sit here my heart is so full with thankfulness. When I look over my life and see all that you have brought me through, I realize I am not even supposed to be here.

I had too many people that spoke many different things over my life, but this goes to show that you have the final say in all things concerning your children.

What the devil meant for bad you will surely turn it round and use it for good.

As I embark on this journey of Eldership, I know you will give me everything I need to complete this assignment.

Amen.

Latrea Wyche

Dear God,

I choose to disconnect from all distractions to draw closer to you. Let my eyes be steady on what you have for me. Help me to never lose focus of the things of substance that produce life.

Amen.

Latrea Wyche

Dear God,

Help me to honor you, as I struggle to draw closer to you during this season of fasting and prayer. Even through persecution use all my conduct to glorify you. In the name of Jesus help me intercede on the behalf of others who may be dealing with judgment, jealously and other unwanted attacks.

Amen.

Dear God,

Please help me to surround myself with people that will always point me toward your best. Today as I fast and seek you, I ask you to give revelation to the people that you have placed in my life, that they will help me to become the person you are calling me to be.

Amen.

Latrea Wyche

Dear God,

I come to you with gladness in my spirit and thanksgiving in my heart. Thanking you for all that you have done and are continuing to do in my life. God, thank you for this 21 day fast that has allowed me not to only grow closer to you, but it gave me an ear to hear.

This fast has also taught me some lessons about your word and principles. One important thing that I learned is "faith without works is dead." I have heard it before, but I never really understood what it meant until after this fast. We pray and ask you to remove things from our lives and your will be done. We being your children have to put in some work as well.

Amen.

Latrea Wyche

Dear God,

I come to you this morning with such joy in my heart. You have blessed me in measures that I cannot even begin to explain. And I just want to say thank you because you did not have to do it, but you did because of your love. This just reminds me to hold on to God's unchanging hand and never let go despite what things looks like.

Amen.

Latrea Wyche

Dear God,

I come to you as humble as I know how. First thanking you for allowing me to see another day and for your glorious presence for allowing just one more breath of your air.

Lord tonight it is my prayer that you continue to bless me and my family. Bless me on my job, keep my haters behind me and allow your words to be my words.

Amen.

Latrea Wyche

Dear God,

As I approach the end of another fast, I rejoice for all lessons that I have gained for clearing the branches of confusion and for bringing peace to a certain situation. Lord this fast has truly shed light on a lot of things for me, it has returned my joy and taught me to have patience.

The funny thing about this is I always considered myself a pretty patient person, but I have come to realize that I am not as patient as I perceive myself to be.

I know with your guidance I shall be all that you have called me to be.

Amen.

Dear God,

I am tired of feeling like I am praying for the same thing or that I am asking forgiveness for the same sin. I feel like Paul when he asked God to remove the throne from his flesh. You told him that your grace was sufficient.

What does that mean?

Do we continue to sin just because we have Grace?

This is not what grace is about. Grace is for those who are trying their best to live by the principles of God.

Amen.

Dear God,

I ask you this morning that you fill me up with your joy, a joy that cannot be explained and that cannot be taken by man. Lord, I want to be set on fire with your Holy Spirit. I want a renewing of my mind. Lord I am asking for a change. I am tired of doing things that I know is against your will.

Amen.

Latrea Wyche

Dear God,

I thank you for your faithfulness. You know what I am capable of even when I am not sure of myself and my direction. You saw what I could not bring myself to see. When I did not believe I was enough you knew I was enough. When I could barely lift my head up out of despair, you were right there.

You continue to plant seeds of faith in my heart by continuously telling me, "This is going to get better, just hold on to my word."

That is a promise that I will continue to hold in my heart.

Amen.

Latrea Wyche

Dear God,

Today I come to you as humbly as I know how. First thanking you for being who you are in my life. I thank you for your precious Holy Spirit and your grace that covers me daily.

This morning I read in your word, "...I tell you, ask and it will be given to you; seek, and you will find; knock, and it will be opened to you.... to the one who knocks it will be opened." **(Luke 11:9-10 ESV)**

I am taking this verse to mean that whatever I ask in your name shall be given because I have the power to move mountains.

Today in your son's name I am asking for peace and joy that can only be found in you. I want you to fill me up with your peace and love that there's no room for anything else.

Amen.

Dear God,

In the name of Jesus, I declare right now that I am free from lust and addiction to pornography.

Lord your word says who the son sets free is free indeed.

I am led by your spirit therefore I do not fulfill the evil desires of the flesh. I will never again be entangled in lustful thoughts or actions.

Your anointing, your burden-removing yoke-destroying power has released me from this sin for good, in Jesus name.

Amen.

Latrea Wyche

Dear God,

Father, I thank you that today I am free from the spirit of lust. I no longer think lustful thoughts, but instead I will think on things that are true, things that will walk in complete victory as self-control over my mind and body in Jesus name.

Amen.

Reflection on Deliverance

The craziest thing about these last two prayers is when I first started praying them, I was still fighting the sin of lust. It was like I was begging God to deliver me from this sin like He was holding me captive or something. God was saying that the deliverance was there for me, but there were some things that I had to do for this to happen.

I wanted to be delivered, but I did not want to give up the things God was telling me to give up to be free.

They felt good to my flesh, but my spirit man was slowly dying because I was not in the will of God for my life.

I remember during this time always saying that I know God has something better for me, but I just did not know how to tap into it.

It was a long road.

Some people I had to let go. There were things I had to stop doing, but I'm happy to report that as of August 2016 I have begun my journey of being lust free.

Is it easy? No. I have been on this journey before, but I was not truly committed like I am now.

It would be like I would start out on the right track, but something would happen that would throw me off.

I got tired of praying for deliverance from the same thing every six months so I just stopped praying.

That was just like handing my soul over to the devil!

Finally understand that God will deliver you, but two things must happen:

One, you must be truly seeking deliverance.

Two, you must be willing to do your part in the process.

There are moments where I get lonely and my mind wants to go back. When that happens, I pray and ask God to direct my mind.

Plus, I have those who are willing to pray for me and with me.

Latrea Wyche

"God answers prayers based on our future not our current situations."

-Latrea Wyche

Latrea Wyche

Unanswered Prayers

Where do unanswered prayers go? A crazy question, right?

All prayers get answered in one form or another, at least that's what I thought.

When God dropped this in my spirit, I was like, "God you gonna have people thinking I am crazy talking about unanswered prayers."

Then He showed me that it's all about people and their perceptions when it comes to whether a prayer is answered or not.

Let me explain.

So many times when we pray, we are praying based on our current situation or our current circumstances.

However, in most cases God answers prayers based on where He is trying to take us.

It took me so long to understand this concept because like most on this journey I used to wonder why certain prayers got answered and certain prayers didn't.

For example, I had been praying for another child for what felt like forever, but God never saw fit to bless me with another one and I always wondered why.

As time moved on, I started having trouble in my marriage and other things started popping up that would not have been conducive to me bringing another child into the world. I guess you could say that was an unanswered prayer.

What we have to come to understand is God know the tests and trials that we are going be faced with. He knows the challenges that are going to come down the line to test our faith. That is the information that God uses when he decides which prayers to answer.

You may pray for a bigger house or a new car, but where He is taking you requires that you save your money.

So God tells you that you don't need a bigger house or new car right now because where He wants to take you there are certain things that you are going to have to have in place and you are not going to have these things in place if you spend your money on houses and cars.

There are those times when God may not answer the prayer the way *you* wanted Him to, so you decide He didn't answer you because He did not fix it the way *you* wanted him to.

We as the people of God need to understand that He is going to bless where He gets glory from.

For example, you may be praying for a place to live and there could be a certain area that you want to live in.

God says, "No, you can't afford it," but He blesses you with something just as nice. However, instead of thanking Him for the blessing, you get hung up on the fact that it was not what *you* wanted.

Why are we so impatient when it comes to prayer?

I am telling you that sometimes we can be the most impatient group of people. We act like God is *a genie in a bottle* or something and He is supposed to grant our every wish when *we* demand it.

God blesses us based on His agenda for our life not ours.

Just because you have been praying for something and you have not heard from God that does not mean that He is not going to answer it.

But He is never going to give you something that He knows is going to be bad for you in the long run or it's not going to bring glory to Him, in some way.

He's going to bless you with something that He knows that you are ready to handle and the responsibility that comes along with whatever you are asking for.

That tends to the problem. Sometimes, when we pray, especially for ourselves we never weigh the cost.

How is this going to affect others around us and is it going to bring glory to God?

These are some of the things that God takes into consideration when answering our prayers.

Dear God,

In the name of Jesus, I declare that I have a blood-brought right to answered prayer. The word of God is my guarantee. Father by prayer and supplication I request and with thanksgiving I can make my request known to you. You hear the prayers of the righteous and answer them. Your eyes are on me and your ears are open to hearing my prayers in Jesus name.

Amen.

Reflection on Praying

I have no clue of what I was going through when I was praying that previous prayer.

I sound confused and was using a bunch of "Godly words," but not really saying anything. It is like that sometimes.

You find yourself saying whatever you feel you need to say to get God's attention.

This is why having a real relationship with God is so important, because regardless of how crazy you think you may sound, God knows your heart.

He knows what you stand in need of, even when you can't communicate it properly.

Intimate Conversations ...

Conclusion

Surrender

This book was a very difficult book to write for several reasons. First, when you are speaking about God, you want to be sure that what you are saying is in line with His word and not something you have heard or made up, especially when talking about something so important as prayer.

Another reason this book was so difficult to write is because I wanted to be obedient to the Holy Spirit, but at the same time I did not want it to sound crazy. It was like I was fighting a battle between my spirit and flesh.

Finally, I decided to totally release the writing process over to the Holy Spirit.

It is my prayer that this book gives you a greater understanding of prayer and the importance of it.

About the Author

Latrea Wyche is 37 years old, originally from PG County MD, she is a life coach and a motivational speaker and a published author. She currently resides in Fayetteville, NC with her husband and their ten year old daughter. Latrea was born with Phiffer Syndrome; a rare genetic disorder that causes the bones in the skull and other parts of the body to not fuse properly, as well as vision and hearing impairment. Latrea has endured more than 30-45 operations to correct various health problems.

Latrea has also had to deal with major family issues such as drug addicted parents. Yet through it all she has managed to defy the odds; earning a

BA in Psychology and a Master's in Education.

Blessed with the God-given ability to empower and motivate people with disabilities, Latrea strives to see people not only find their voice but use their voice to live their best life, find their purpose but most importantly learn the importance of being real with themselves.

Facebook:
www.facebook.com/coachLatrea

Twitter:
https://twitter.com/coachlatrea

Email:
coachlatreawyche@gmail.com

Instagram:
https://www.instagram.com/coachlatrea79/

YouTube:
https://www.youtube.com/channel/UCFLWR0q1XDY9zjwgeThfrIg

The Butterfly Typeface Publishing

The Butterfly Typeface Publishing House Company is a full service professional publishing company. Our goal is to 'spread a message' of inspiration, imagination and intrigue in all that we do.

Whether you hire us to edit, ghostwrite, publish (books & magazines) or web design, you can be guaranteed exemplary customer service, fairness and quality.

Our vision, under God's leadership, is to serve and assist in the healing of the heart, mind and soul of *all* people we encounter with integrity, intentional influence and positive purpose.

"We make good GREAT!"

Iris M. Williams – Owner

The Butterfly Typeface Publishing House Co

PO Box 56193

Little Rock Arkansas 72215

www.butterflytypeface.com